FOCUS ON THE FAMILY ®

HELP!
MY ADULT CHILD WON'T LEAVE HOME

HELP!
MY ADULT CHILD WON'T LEAVE HOME

dr. bill maier
general editor

stephen bly
author

Tyndale House Publishers, Inc.
Carol Stream, Illinois

Help! My Adult Child Won't Leave Home
Copyright © 2006 by Stephen A. Bly
All rights reserved. International copyright secured.

This book is excerpted and adapted from *Once a Parent, Always a Parent* © 1993
by Stephen Bly.

A Focus on the Family book published by
Tyndale House Publishers, Carol Stream, Illinois 60188

TYNDALE and Tyndale's quill logo are registered trademarks of Tyndale House
Publishers, Inc.

Edited by Kathy Davis and Liz Duckworth
Cover designed by Joseph Sapulich
Cover photograph © by Paul Edmondson/Getty Images. All rights reserved.

Library of Congress Cataloging-in-Publication Data
Bly, Stephen A., 1944-
  Help! my adult child won't leave home / by Stephen A. Bly ; Bill Maier, general
editor.
     p. cm.
  A Focus on the family book.
  This book is excerpted and adapted from Once a parent, always a parent,
© 1993 by Stephen Bly.
  Includes bibliographical references and index.
  ISBN-13: 978-1-58997-174-5 (alk. paper)
  ISBN-10: 1-58997-174-4 (alk. paper)
  1. Parent and adult child. 2. Intergenerational relations. I. Maier, Bill.
II. Bly, Stephen A., 1944- Once a parent, always a parent. III. Title.
HQ755.86.B594 2006
646.7'8—dc22

                              2006013553

Printed in the United States of America
1 2 3 4 5 6 7 8 9 / 11 10 09 08 07 06

Contents

Foreword

Tim and Karen are an active couple in their mid-fifties with three grown kids. They've saved their money and invested well over the years, and Tim is planning to take an early retirement. They're looking forward to serving on a one-year medical mission project in Indonesia.

Last week they received a panicked call from their 27-year-old daughter, Kim, who lives in California. Kim shared that her five-year marriage is on the rocks and she has left her husband. In addition, the corporation she works for has just announced a major layoff, leaving her jobless. She was calling her parents to ask if she can move back home and live with them—beginning next week.

Millions of American families have adult children living at home, and the phenomenon is growing. Sociologists call them "boomerang kids"—young adults who either continue living at home after high school or college or return to live with their parents after living on their own for a time. The reasons are as varied as the personalities of the kids.

If you've suddenly found yourself in a position similar to Tim and Karen's, you've come to the right place. Stephen Bly's book will help you navigate the sometimes rough waters that families experience when adult children and their parents live in the same household. He'll teach you how to determine if the living arrangement is a healthy one, how to negotiate appropriate limits and boundaries, and how to determine when it's time to gently push an adult child "out of the nest." He'll also address difficult issues such as when to evict an adult child because of destructive behaviors. Along the way, he'll provide you with some key spiritual insights through the parable of the prodigal son.

We hope you'll find this book to be a helpful resource as you attempt to strike a balance between love and limits in your relationship with your adult child.

Dr. Bill Maier
Vice President, Psychologist in Residence
Focus on the Family

The Crowded Nest:
When Adult
Children Live
at Home

J ason lives down the street and drives a black '65 Corvette that he keeps shined to mirror perfection. Every Friday and Saturday night, he takes the 'vette into the city and cruises 21st Street. To maintain the expense of repairs, insurance, and general upkeep of such a rig, Jason works at odd jobs around town. He house-sits, paints barns, and drives a truck during harvest.

Sounds like an industrious 17-year-old with expensive tastes, doesn't he?

But Jason is 31 years old and still lives at home with his parents, Matt and Sherry. He has attended seven different colleges, never spending more than a couple of months at any of them. He's had great jobs, lousy jobs, but mostly no jobs. Matt pays the light bill, the mortgage, and for groceries. Jason, when he has the money, pays for the cable TV.

Five times Jason left home to begin an

independent life; five times he returned. Matt and Sherry sometimes feel resigned, sometimes angry, and sometimes like failures. Often they just feel trapped.

ၐ ၐ ၐ

Trisha was a junior in college, living 900 miles from home, when she decided to get married—to a divorced man 10 years her senior. Her parents tried to persuade her to wait until after graduation. They warned her that it would be difficult. They cautioned her about dropping out of school. They described how tough life can be in the big city.

Three years, two children, and countless bruises and black eyes later, Trisha and the kids took the Greyhound bus back to her parents' house. Dad now pays the bills, and Mom works at the insurance company until noon, then baby-sits the kids. Trisha returned to college and is working toward a teaching degree. She spends every day at school and every evening doing homework.

The nest is more than full—it's crowded.

ᘯ ᘯ ᘯ

Whether our adult children live at home, across town, or across the country, we parents fill a unique role in their lives. Our roles will change and vary with age and circumstances, but we will always be parents. And our job is never finished. In a sense, because we will always be Mom and Dad, we will always be "parenting."

Up to this point, we have interjected our parenting into our children's lives in decreasing levels of intensity. But from this point on, we must stop altogether. The adult child must now determine when and where our love, wisdom, and skills are needed.

Few parents nowadays complain about the crisis of an empty nest. Rather, they shudder at the thought that the nest will never become empty. Maybe you're thinking the same thing, and that's why you picked up this book. We'll look at how to handle destructive behavior and when and how to move an adult child out, but we'll also consider how to make the arrangement work if your child has to live with you awhile longer. This book is about:

- real moms and dads,
- real adult children,
- none perfect,
- and, at times, all in less-than-ideal situations.

A number of interesting acronyms have developed to describe this situation. Maybe what you need at home is PRI—you know, Premarital Residential Independence.[1]

Many parents face the dreaded afflic-
tion of RYAS—Returning Young Adult
Syndrome.[2]

And then there's my favorite, ILYA.
Some communities are littered with
ILYAs—Incompletely-Launched Young
Adults.[3]

Or, in terms you and I can understand,
"The kids are still at home! What do I do
now?" Or, "Help! Our kids moved back
home!"

First, if you have adult children at
home, relax! It's a common phenomenon.
According to an article on the Web site
SeniorJournal.com:

> Twenty-five percent of Baby Boomers
> anticipate their adult children will
> move back in with them. Of Boomers
> polled, 15 percent have grown children

who already returned to the nest. Called "boomerang kids," this is a growing social phenomenon.

Julie Tillson, 57, a high school teacher and resident of Del Webb's Sun City Lincoln Hills in Northern California, has experienced the boomerang phenomenon firsthand. After going away to college for several years, her daughter returned home. "Stephanie moved back in with us for three months," Tillson said. "She needed to because of financial reasons. It was horrible at first. She felt like a failure and it was hard. But by the time she moved out again, we were sorry to see her go."

Today more than 25 percent of Americans ages 18 to 34 live with their parents, according to U.S. Census fig-

ures. For 18- to 24-year-olds, 56 percent of men and 43 percent of women
live with one or both parents. These
numbers may increase too. According
to a job search Web site, 62 percent of
college students say they expect to live
at home after graduation.[4]

Second, if you have adult children at
home, don't apologize for it. It's not necessarily a sign of failure. Success is not
determined by economic good fortune,
scholastic achievements, social popularity,
or how rapidly or slowly children pull
away from their parents.

Why Adult Children Come Home

In recent years, several social factors have
contributed to the fact that more and more
adult children live at home.

Economics

"Most boom-era parents had the economic winds at their back," writes Liz Pulliam Weston. "They graduated into a decent job market and enjoyed strong appreciation of their homes and (for the most part) stock portfolios. Today's graduates, by contrast,

ༀ ༀ ༀ

"Our single, 30-year-old daughter moved back home last April. She couldn't find meaningful work in Denver, after being there for nearly five years, so we didn't mind having her return. She stays in our basement apartment and pays $300 a month for rent. Yes, we could use the money from a regular tenant, but she is quiet and keeps the place clean. She is working and paying off student loans. I'm happy she has a safe place to stay, but it has been an adjustment."

are a bit more behind the eight ball: The economy is far from robust, meaning more 20-somethings are unemployed or under-employed. Instead of getting free money in the form of grants to pay for college, they're taking out student loans—an aver-age of about $20,000 at last count. And then there's the Demon Credit Card. . . . The median credit card debt for undergrad-uates has risen by 32 percent since 1998, to $3,730, according to a Nellie Mae study."[5]

In some fields, an overabundance of college graduates is applying for a limited number of job openings. This means employers can be selective and demand even more stringent training. That trans-lates into graduate school, spiraling educa-tion costs, increased college indebtedness, doubled independent housing expenses, and more kids needing to stay with Mom and Dad . . . just a few more years.

Marriage Deterioration

After years of living in a society where divorce is presented as an agreeable alternative to working through difficult situations, many adult children more quickly jump to divorce or separation as the best solution available. The results of turbulent, broken relationships lead adult children to seek a place that provides security, stability, and acceptance. The natural inclination is to go home.

Frank Furedi, sociology professor at the University of Kent, adds: "In contrast to the insecurities attached to adult relationships, the security of the parental home can appear attractive. In these circumstances, the aspiration of young adults for autonomy can be diminished. Some young adults embrace a delayed phase of dependency, as independence becomes associated with unpredictable risks. . . .

Many young adults who manage to move out of the family home end up constituting a rapidly growing group of singletons. Being single has become a way of life for millions of men and women in their twenties and thirties. . . . In the USA singletons are the fastest growing demographic group."[6]

The Push toward Quality Careers

Only a few decades ago, most folks were satisfied with a job that paid the bills and provided stability. Now, such employment is touted as inferior. A job must be personally fulfilling. It must challenge the inner person. It must be an extension and expression of your own essence. It must lead to upward advancement. It must be exciting. Careers like that are sometimes hard to find.

Brett spent nine years driving a cement

truck. On his twenty-seventh birthday, he realized he wanted more out of life. He moved back home and is taking art classes at the university. If you ask Brett, he'll tell about someday having his own studio and gallery. If you talk to his folks, they'll tell you they don't have a clue how long Brett will be living with them.

The Comfort-of-Home Factor

Let's face it. Some of us just might be reaping the rewards of our success. We worked hard to make our homes safe, comfortable, relaxed, enjoyable retreats for our children while they grew up in a rather frightening and hostile world. Now that they have reached adult age, some children are in no hurry to abandon the comfort of the world we have created for them.

Nels and Germaine worked hard to fix up the rather run-down home they inherited from Germaine's parents. By making a lot of sacrifices, they were able to turn the place into a showcase. They added a swimming pool and built a one-room cabana next to it, complete with mini-kitchen, game room, and bathroom.

Their son, Jensen, has been the produce manager at the supermarket for three years. He had supposedly been looking for his own place, but he can't find anything that compares to the poolside cabana at home. Chances are he never will.

The Extension of Adolescence

"Society has come to accept the idea that people do not become adults until they are in their late thirties. As a result, adolescence has been extended well into the twenties."[7]

"Anglo-American culture is ambiguous in its response to this development. The occasional outcry against some absurd manifestation of this trend is drowned out by the powerful message that growing up is a troublesome and unpleasant activity."[8]

Professor Furedi provides this example: "Fred Simons and Oliver Bailer, both real estate agents in their late twenties, play with their Nintendo and boast that they haven't changed much since their school years. Helen Timerman, a 27-year-old designer, proudly shows me her collection of soft toys. She loves cuddling them and believes that her little animals, neatly arranged in her bedroom, give her a zone of security."[9]

Six Problems to Anticipate When Adult Children Return Home

Obviously, having adult children move back home won't always be smooth sailing. But it's not unrealistic to expect that since it's your home, you have the right to set the rules. Of course there should be discussion and negotiation, but the final say belongs to you, the parent and homeowner. This includes issues such as noise, cleanliness, visits by friends (especially those of the opposite sex), and so on. It also includes the question of how much time you'll dedicate to baby-sitting your grandchildren, if your adult child has children. You are under no obligation to provide a free baby-sitting service with no limits, unless that is your choice.

With those issues and others like them in mind, in the next section we'll discuss

ϑ ϑ ϑ

"I've had to go into counseling over this situation. A family of five . . . both parents and three kids . . . is just too much. They've been living with me more than two years now!"

___ ૭ ૭ ૭ ___

"Our adult son has moved back in but does not contribute much to household expenses, and we help him out financially at times. We enjoy having him around, but his progress has taken a year so far and my husband and I argue about whether we're on the right track. We take turns wanting to throw him out and tell him to figure it out like we had to do. He lacks essential skills and education, which makes it really hard for us all. We do notice the financial drain when we postpone buying big-ticket items and taking additional vacations. We don't want to kick him out if all he needs is a few more months to get on his feet. But there are no indicators we can see to say what his and our status is on the scale of 'progress' and 'moving ahead.'"

communication and negotiation. But first let's look at some common problems that occur when generations live together under one roof.

Arguments

"Because I'm the mother and I say so. That's why!" That statement doesn't end the discussion when children are 29 the way it did when they were nine. You may argue over who's responsible for washing the sheets and who's going to pick up the grandchildren's toys in the living room. Chances are, your pattern of settling differences with your adult children will be similar to what it was when they were teenagers.

Increased Need for Privacy

Your child may be trying to redirect his life and find a new job, establish new relationships, and set new goals. Those are important matters that need serious "think time"—quiet, private moments. Parents also need privacy.

Continuing Sibling Rivalry

If you have other children at home when an adult child moves back, you'll have an easier time handling the crowded nest.[10] But there will be sibling rivalry between your resident children and your returning adult child.

Disagreement over Finances

There will be times when you and your spouse don't agree on how to spend your money, especially when the expenses are related to your adult child. And you'll have plenty of discussions on how your adult children spend (or don't spend) their money. Many major blowouts are over minor items.

Extra Tension between Mom and Dad

Parents seldom totally agree over what to do when an adult child wants to move back home. They might not agree on whether they should allow him to move back at all, and they probably have few agreements over what the rules should be

---

೦ ೦ ೦

"Since my son and his family moved back in, I've been faced with massive repair bills for broken windows, doors, screens, the garage door, fixing holes in walls. They don't help with the housework . . . not even taking out the garbage. I'm going to sell and move out to a seniors-only complex."

once he does move back in. This holds true for an adult child who has never left home as well.

Most often, it seems, fathers see resident adult children as some sort of failure, while mothers view them as kids who still need mothering. There will probably be a number of arguments between the parents over the adult child.

Serious Strain in Households with Returning Stepchildren and in Single-Parent Households

For many, the years of conflict with young stepchildren can be tolerated because parents hope for relief when stepchildren reach the age to seek independent residence. But what if the stepchild doesn't move out? Or what if he moves back home?

The stepparent situation often strains

the marital relationship between Mom and Stepdad (or vice versa) to a breaking point. "He's your kid!" becomes the battle cry.

In a single-parent situation, a returning child can cause an emotional and financial burden almost too great to bear. Most often, children who return home to a single parent return to the mother.

Making
Living
Together
Work for
Everyone

With all the conflicts that can occur within a crowded nest, it might seem it is something to be avoided at all costs. But that isn't necessarily true. While always striving for the goal of independence for our children, we can still enjoy the benefits that come along with the strain of having an adult child at home. For most of us, the benefits outweigh the struggles. Families can grow stronger and closer together through this experience.

Strengthening the Family

Following are four keys to assure a strengthened family that includes resident adult children.

1. *Talk more but don't yell.*

Establish a regular channel of communication through which all household residents can express their thanks and air their gripes. Rather than wait for things to burst apart, parents should initiate the discussion.

Weekly family council meetings might be a forum for you. For instance, every Thursday night at seven o'clock, the family may turn off the television and computer, sit down, and talk about how things are going. Any subject can be discussed, and any suggestion offered.

You can tell your adult daughter that it is her responsibility to scrub the bath-

---

Ͻ Ͻ Ͻ

"Two families in one house has its problems, but also its rewards. I loved the family dinners and birthdays. I loved the togetherness with my grandchildren. Other cultures have extended families, so why does our culture make it out to be such a horrible problem? It can be wonderful for the children."

room fixtures in her bathroom. And she can add that she doesn't feel it's necessary to inform you where she is every minute of the day. Talk about days off, vacations, phone bills, automobile use, credit cards, late-staying friends, suitable DVDs, and other necessities of life.

But no yelling. No insults. Just open talk, with every member of the household getting a chance to state his or her ideas. Universally, it seems, arguments that include yelling quickly lead to disintegration of the parent/adult child relationship.

A family council meeting might sound a tad hokey at first, but a solid commitment to such an activity will reap helpful, honest communication.

2. Divide the tasks and expenses.

"When adult children remain or return home, parent and child must negotiate roles and responsibilities in the context of a shared household," say researchers.[11]

Jot down a list of recurring tasks needed to make the house function:

washing the clothes
cooking
cleaning (general)
cleaning (room-by-room)
washing the cars
sweeping the garage
building a fire
taking out the trash
mowing the lawn
doing the dishes
changing the linens
feeding the pets

On and on your list might go. You get the idea. Then work through the entire list with your resident adult child until you all agree who will have primary responsibility for each one of the tasks.

It's wise to name a backup person for each chore as well. For instance, if you agree that it's the mother's task to cook supper, then you might want to appoint the resident adult daughter as backup. This means that if Mom is gone next Tuesday night to a meeting, she, and everyone else, knows that the daughter is in charge of feeding the family.

Some of these things might seem petty and obvious, but it's unlikely that many

ↄ ↄ ↄ

"I would like to have my children live with me for the company and because I love to be with them, but only if they pay half the house payment and the cost of their own food. I'll share the cooking and cleaning, but I won't do all of it. It can work, but only if everybody does his or her part."

families often discuss such items, and it is the little things that can cause the problems. If the delegation of jobs does not seem fair, it needs to be sincerely discussed and the chore list updated at a family council meeting.

3. Plan together where all of this is leading.

It is important to discuss what the long-term goals might be for the present living condition. Here are some questions to consider:

- Is your adult child going to stay at home until marriage or remarriage?
- Is there an educational goal to complete?
- Will your child need a job that pays a certain amount before being able to leave?

- Will your child set up an independent residence only when you have enough income to establish it?
- How will everyone know when it's time for your child to move on?
- Will it be acceptable for you to leave the whole matter open-ended?

Having a plan does not guarantee it will be completed. But it does unite all parties in a common goal. Plans do change. So keep talking about those new plans until they become clear.

4. *Spend time playing together.*

How do you play with a 29-year-old son? Find a way. "Co-resident parents and adult children must also negotiate their social interaction, the degree of shared leisure time. Parental satisfaction with co-residence appears to be highest when parents are involved with adult children in pleasurable activities."[12]

Maybe you can join your adult child in snowboarding or skiing, disc golf, basketball, or a Pilates class. Perhaps you could afford to buy a boat so you and your adult daughter can water-ski at the lake. Possibly you and your adult child would enjoy one of the following activities together: a play, a concert, a film, a sporting event, an opera, a swap meet, an auction, a garage sale, a mall opening, a hobby, a vacation, a board game, a television show, a book series, volunteer charity work, a rodeo, or watching a sunset.

You come from different generations, but you live in the same world. Don't allow your home to be a lonely place, merely a room and a bed, for your resident adult child. Search for reasons to accept your children, not for reasons to exclude them.

Look for opportunities to participate in

your children's adventures. Some of them you might not want to do no matter what, but there will be some things you can do together.

Giving Advice in a Healthy Way

Many times your adult children will still need to hear your advice and wisdom. But whether advice is welcome and how much advice your child will accept depend on the personality of each child. Which of these seven categories might your adult child or children fit into? As you read them, consider how you would tailor giving advice to match your child's personality.

1. Fiercely Independent—Lesli never asks her father for advice because that would be admitting a weakness. But that doesn't mean she doesn't need his advice, and it doesn't mean he refuses to give it.

2. Sporadically Opinionated—Darren does not take advice about computers, ski resorts, rap music, Democrats, Russian novels, or the Cleveland Indians. He is, in his mind, an expert on those topics and would be insulted to think his father might know more about any of them. So unless it's a matter of physical harm or unless he's asked a direct question, Darren's dad does not give his son advice on those topics. Everything else is open for discussion.

3. Impetuous Adventurer—DeLynne does listen to her parents' advice on how to get herself out of the tight squeezes her impulsive decisions create. Her parents' role seems to be to help minimize the damage of DeLynne's impetuous adventures.

4. Moody Contemplator—Quin will stew, worry, and be generally depressed until the last possible moment when making a decision. Then he will finally decide. His parents often have nothing to do but listen and wait for the decision. After that, they spend weeks helping Quin be happy with the decision he made.

5. Hard-driving Perfectionist—Angie is a single 29-year-old teacher. Her mother has almost given up telling her daughter to relax, take a vacation, or just kick back a little. She says, "Angie can't back away from her intense quest for excellence. But she still needs me to tell her what a great job she is doing. Angie doesn't need, nor could she accept, my advice. She just needs a mental and physical hug once in a while."

6. Easygoing Procrastinator—Martin has trouble making decisions, and his dad has learned to understand Martin's personality. So he tries to hold back, but does speak out when Martin indicates he would welcome his father's making a decision for him.

7. Timid Pilgrim—When Chelsea was in high school, she wanted to get a job at the music store, but she sat in the car for 30 minutes trying to work up the nerve to apply. Her mother finally made her go. Chelsea got the job and loved it. Upon college graduation, Chelsea landed an interview with a music company in Burbank. Her mom flew to the coast and helped Chelsea find her way around the city. That was eight years ago, and Chelsea's career has progressed nicely. Today she thanks her mom

for the understanding support that has helped her overcome her timidity and achieve her goals.

Tips for Helping Your Child Make Difficult Decisions

There are four things you can tell your adult children about any difficult decision they face:

1. what you did in a similar circumstance;
2. the facts or where to find the facts;
3. not to do anything until they reach complete agreement with their mate (if they are married);
4. to choose the option that will produce the best result in the long run.

Remember one last point as you share wisdom with older children: They may have some good advice for you, too. You'll be more effective as a parental counselor if you are in the habit of receiving advice. Always consult them in their area of expertise. Publicly compliment them when you followed their advice and the results were positive. Don't criticize or even joke when their advice turns out to be wrong. Allow them to reteach you the lessons you once taught them.

Lending or Giving Money without Going Broke

We want our adult kids to be financially independent and pay their own way. Also,

---

ʘ ʘ ʘ

"When my daughter moved back home, she wanted to be treated as a child and have everything done for her instead of acting like an adult and taking responsibility, or even sharing the costs of the household."

as much as possible, we want to avoid putting a strain on our own finances. After all, we don't owe our kids a bailout. But the situation can get sticky when our kids seem to be in financial need. Here are some factors that can help you keep a clear head when you are considering whether to offer financial help to your adult children.

Get yourself in good financial shape first.

Your own disastrous economic conditions will leave you with few resources for helping anyone else. Very few of us will ever be wealthy, but we can aim for stability. Don't put yourself in dire financial straits.

Uphold a sound view of money.

Your adult children may question why you handle your finances the way you do, or they might seek advice for how they should

establish their own family finances. You
need to be ready to respond with more than
a hunch or a theory. Following sound financial principles keeps your policies from
being subjective and helps establish them
upon something more solid than present
circumstances and momentary disasters.

ꧏ ꧏ ꧏ

"I do believe that grown returning children
should pay for half the cost of housing,
utilities, and expenses, as well as babysit-
ting. Have them sit down with the bills and
split them with you. If they won't do this,
tell them you can't afford the extra expense
of having them there, and to get their own
place. Housework should be divided up
too. This was the biggest problem I had.
My family thought I should do it all since it
was my house."

There's a lot more to money than just getting more of it. And there's more to family life than trying to take care of every monetary need your adult children might have. Parents should not be seen as the cavalry, ready to rescue adult children from every financial pinch. Our kids need to learn to pay their way, budget their funds, and live within their means.

Make sure you and your mate completely agree.
Here are a few guidelines:

- Don't give or lend money if it has the potential for causing sibling contempt.
- Don't call the money a loan if you both know your child can't possibly repay it.
- Conduct all your discussions about the financial loan or gift in private with your mate.

Don't give or loan money you don't have.
When you just don't have money to
spare, or when you think assisting with
money is the wrong thing to do, help
your child find another solution. For
example, you might help her get a bank
loan, suggest that she get a second job, or
help her find a way to barter or exchange
goods or labor.

***Distinguish clearly between gifts
and loans.***
Gifts should be gifts with no strings
attached and no payments due. You can
give the recipients your vast wisdom about
investing the gift, but it's all theirs.

Everyone needs to be clear whether it
will be a gift or a loan. It is extremely
important that everyone understands the
arrangement. And don't feel bad or guilty
if you have to insist on a loan because you

need the money to be repaid—or you just *want* it to be repaid. Remember, it's *your* money unless you choose to give it away.

Loans should be documented on paper. Actually, you can set whatever minimum figure you'd like. Maybe in your economic condition, you need it in writing if it's over $20. Or perhaps it's no big deal to you until it's over $1,000. The point is, loans should be based on more than just the fading memory of a verbal agreement.

Annually, the lender should send to the borrower a statement listing how much

---

૭ ૭ ૭

"I have just put my house up for sale because I feel like a prisoner in my own home. The cost of repairing the damage done by the grandchildren is outrageous. The disrespect I receive is terrible."

money was paid on the loan during the year, how much went to interest, and how much went to principal. The right kind of form can be secured from your banker, a friend at a real estate office, or various computer programs and Web sites.

Saying No to Your Adult Children without Slamming the Door

Tal and Lannae lived in a little 1930s bungalow for 15 years before they could afford to build a nicer house nearby. After years of scrimping and saving, it was a dream come true. Their kids are grown now, and the house is peaceful and a joy to the couple. There's room for the whole gang when they bring their families for a visit.

Their 28-year-old daughter, Shana, is expecting her third child, and she and her husband have a little bungalow in the same city. But their two-bedroom place is getting cramped and they need a larger home. They can afford a bigger house only in an undesirable neighborhood.

For months, Shana was anxious over what to do. Finally she came upon the "perfect" solution. She proposed to her parents, "Since you like to travel more and don't want to spend all your time on such a big place, why don't you two move into our bungalow, and we'll move into your bigger place? It would be such a great home for raising kids!"

That's an easy no, you say. But not if Shana is your daughter. Not if those three adorable children are your grandkids!

"What about it, Mom and Dad? Will you trade houses?"

"Dad, can I borrow $4,000 for a new motorcycle?"

"Daddy, can't you get Larry a job at your office?"

We all have times when we just have to say no. Some decisions are quite simple. Many are not. Do three important things before you give your answer:

1. *Listen.* Make sure you've heard the whole story.
2. *Think.* Ask, "How much time do I have to think about this before you need an answer?" Up to some obvious limits, the more time spent considering a situation, the better the decision will be.
3. *Discuss.* Talk over the situation carefully with your mate. The best answer will convince both of you.

Six Characteristics of a Nice No

If you decide that your answer has to be no, you'll want to say it in a way that will preserve the relationship. The following guidelines will help you do that.

1. Be reasonable. Your answer should come with good reasons to support it, and you should be open to reasonable questions.[13] For example, when Shana asks Tal and Lannae to exchange houses with her family, they might calmly explain to Shana that they worked hard and sacrificed for many years to have a house that would suit their needs and hold all the children and grandchildren.

2. Be gentle. A gentle no is one that will probably not anger your children. It has the feeling of tenderness and compassion. This might mean that Tal and Lannae would express genuine concern over Shana's housing dilemma and sympathy that her growing family feels crowded.

3. Be distinct. Make your yes indisputable. Make your no crystal clear. Tal and Lannae should make it clear that yes, they understand Shana's problem, but no, they are not going to exchange houses.

4. *Be uplifting.* This means that your words should add to another person's moral, intellectual, or spiritual improvement. Here's the twist. You need to consider how saying no to your adult children helps them understand you and themselves bet-

---

ƍ ƍ ƍ

"We sat down and composed a list of house rules for our adult child . . . the things we could stand to live with. We pay the bills, so we make the rules. The 'child' took a look at them (curfews, job requirements, random drug test, room searches, etc.) and said 'No thanks!' We made a pact between us (my husband and I) that we would stand firm on our rules, and we communicated that to our adult child."

ter. Perhaps Tal and Lannae should remind Shana that they lived in a cramped house when she and her siblings were growing up, and the family was able to work around it and grow from the challenges.

5. *Exhibit peace and strength.* Remember that peace and strength are much more than just the absence of conflict. *Peace* is confident assurance that God is still in control in the midst of conflict. *Strength* is the ability to endure a tough situation and come out of it stronger than you were before. Both characteristics assume conflict and trial. Tal and Lannae can assume that by remaining peaceful and strong, their relationship with their daughter will be preserved and even strengthened.

6. *Be concerned about long-term goals.* Long after I'm gone, I want my son to be an example to his children, his grand-children, and his grandchildren's children.

That's my goal for his life. And any decision I am allowed to have in his life now should reflect that ongoing goal.

Tal and Lannae might consider that giving Shana their house could cause her to expect that in the future everything should easily work out her way. Refusing her request this time will increase her ability to face challenges now and in the future.

Dealing with Your Adult Child's Struggles

When your adult child can't seem to get his act together and take responsibility for his life, some common emotions surface.

First, it's important to set aside your emotions.

Two common emotions—resentment and failure—fight to possess your thoughts during times of stress. You will feel resentment: Why is my child doing this to me? After all we did for her, she is self-centered and spoiled. She is going her merry way, and we have to pay the price.

And you will feel failure: If we had done the job right the first time, if we'd sent him to military school, if we hadn't sent him to military school, if I'd helped him with his math, if I'd been there when he needed me, if we'd insisted that he not date that girl, if we hadn't moved during his senior year, if . . . if . . . if . . .

☾ ☾ ☾

"I can't believe I had to serve an eviction notice on my own children to get them out. Now they are furious with me and say I'll never get to see the grandkids again."

Set realistic goals.

Struggling children do not always move back home, but they all need to find a new direction in life. So with you and your spouse advising, help them set realistic goals.

A realistic goal is one that all of you believe is within reach. A realistic goal is

---
ͻ ͻ ͻ

"I had to tell my grown son who moved back in to pay half the utilities when they doubled and to pay for the damage his children did to the house. Before he moved in I set a deadline for how long the family would stay and insisted he buy the groceries. But the cost of utilities and damage, and the chores that needed to be shared, were not discussed. It created hard feelings when I brought up these new rules."

also measurable. For example, when Richard and Betty's son, Andy, moved back to his parents' home with his children after his wife left them, he set three goals for himself: He would quit drinking, he would take a nine-month vo-tech course in welding, and he and his boys would be in their own home in 18 months. This plan was realistic and measurable.

Plan how to reach those goals.

Goals are not reached overnight. Nor do they happen without plans.

If your daughter needs to get her own place, don't simply say, "Well, Darci is going to move out whenever she finds the right house." Instead, calculate the cost of rental, lease, or purchase. (Include first and last months' rent, cleaning and security deposit, moving cost, or other expenses.) Then estimate how much your daughter can contribute per month to that fund. If it will take five months for her to save enough money, Darci can set a goal: In six months, she will be settled in her own residence.

Agree how you can help.

What do you owe your adult children? Probably nothing. For better or worse, you raised them to adulthood. They are responsible for their own decisions. To claim that their present difficulties are the parents' fault only hinders their progress toward independence.

But you do have an investment of love, and most times you will want to help your struggling adult child get reestablished. So discuss exactly what you see your role to be.

Be specific. Here are a few examples:

- "We will allow you to live at home for two years. You pay for room and board, at $300 per month."
- "We will pay one-half of your rent until the retraining program is completed."
- "We will watch the grandchildren after school every day for one year."
- "We will allow you to use the old pickup until next September so you can save to buy a vehicle."

Set specific, objective points of measurement.

Don't wait until the very end to find out if you reached your goal. Decide on a way to evaluate progress and redefine goals and roles if necessary. Set a date, such as, "On the first of December we will evaluate this arrangement." And establish some performance standards for measurement. If your child is to finish college in two years, for instance, at the end of six months he should have completed 15 or more units of credit. If he is saving to get his own place, he needs $1,000 saved by January 1.

Explain your position if goals are unmet. Explain what your position must be if your child refuses to reach those goals—

ɔ ɔ ɔ

"If a grown child won't bear the burden of paying his way in life, all that can be done is to ask him to leave and fend for himself, or find a shelter to live in. The solution is to get the kid to get a job and pay for half of everything or go to a shelter."

not merely fails to reach, but refuses to reach. Sometimes goals are unreachable. Sometimes circumstances truly prevent goals from being reached. Some goals are dated and lose their value with time.

Fulfill your part of the arrangement.
It might mean working overtime, going back to work, giving up golf, or putting up with a backache every night from lifting the grandkids, but fulfill your part of the arrangement. If you fail to keep your promise, you will spend the rest of your life wondering what it could have been like if you had stuck to the agreement.

Accept the consequences.
No plan, good or poor, always succeeds. Maybe your adult child will suddenly get a life, straighten out his family

relationships, settle down, and live happily ever after. Or he may bomb out again and again and again. Most adult children will probably end up somewhere in between.

Forgiving Adult Children Who Disappoint You

What do you do when adult children reject moral, social, and spiritual wisdom and choose a life that is totally unacceptable? There's just such a story in the New Testament.[14] In this account, a man's younger son asks his father for his share of the estate, then sets off for another country. He squanders his entire inheritance in wild living and eventually ends up in a literal pigpen. Though the details may have changed, this is still a common story today. Let's look at a few things we can learn from the parable of the prodigal son.

Remember, a good environment does not ensure perfect children.[15]

Though the prodigal son left home and made a series of bad choices, there's no indication that his home life was anything substandard or severe.

Since the time of Freud, childhood environment—and specifically parental actions or inactions—have taken the rap for almost everything. Many of us have done a less-than-sterling job in raising our kids. But remember:

- There are no perfect people.[16]
- All people are responsible for their own actions.[17]
- All people (even your children) are capable of totally unreasonable actions.[18]

Geoffrey and Marcia were exemplary citizens with a reputation for honesty, stability, and credibility. That's why it came as a shock when their son, Allen, was arrested for embezzling a large sum of money from the car dealership where he was the accountant. People speculated about where Geoff and Marcia had gone wrong in their parenting. Even Geoff and Marcia struggled to find fault in themselves.

But Allen's problem was all his own. During college he began a secret habit of gambling—poker in the dorms, bets on sporting events, an occasional trip to the casinos. After college, as his income grew, so did his addiction, until he began losing more than he made. He began skimming at work, until finally he was caught. It should have been no more surprising than if it had happened to the son of an alcoholic parent. Behavior does not necessarily reflect home environment.

Eventually we have to allow our adult children to make their own choices.[19] Returning to the story of the prodigal, we never read about the sorrow in the father's heart when he gives his youngest son the inheritance and allows him to run off to the city. But it's not hard to imagine.

Bruce and Amber's son, Ted, had just finished dental school when he announced

---
୨ ୨ ୨

"We still have younger kids at home, and an older child moving back in. We made up a list of rules the adult will have to follow—necessary because he's had drug and alcohol problems. We made random drug testing a rule. The rules don't include rent in our case, but I think they should. They do include having a job."

over the phone, "I'm moving in with a friend while I do my internship."

The friend turned out to be a woman 16 years older than Ted. She had been married three times, had two teenagers, and was a heavy drinker. Ted didn't ask his parents' advice and wasn't interested in their concerns. He simply informed them that he was capable of making his own decisions. He's right, no matter how lousy his decisions might be.

Adult children need to know intuitively that the door to Mom and Dad's home is never completely shut.[20]

What made the prodigal return home and plead for mercy? He knew his dad treated all people kindly.

Ronnie hadn't seen his parents in 12 years, though he called them once or twice a year. One day he called and asked them if he could move home. "Mom, there's no nice way to say this. I have AIDS and I'm dying."

Less than a year later, Ronnie died in his mother's arms in his parents' house—a home where he found an open door.

Adult children need to see an open display of compassion.[21]

Upon his son's return, the prodigal's father threw his arms around the young man, hugged him, and kissed him even before there was any confession of sorrow. It was a very public display of love.

At 21, Heidi flew home from college during her senior year, unmarried and pregnant. Her parents met her at the airport, and the first thing her father did was hug her for about five minutes. Tears flowed and the people in the terminal stared. "I was so scared that I'd come home and you wouldn't want to hug me anymore!" Heidi said. Dad hugged her that day, and he was the first to hug her five months later when the baby arrived.

Truly repentant children, no matter what acts they committed, need our forgiveness. But what about those cases where there is no regret or remorse? This is a tough question. However, you should not let your grown kids get away with inappropriate behavior or wrongdoing. Keep these key principles in mind when you need to discuss your adult children's failures with them:

- We all have times when we need to be confronted for failing to live up to acceptable standards.
- Correct your children with patience and instruction.[22]
- Let them know that you are by no means perfect, but that you do want

to help them overcome their failing
in any way you can.[23]

- Don't make enemies of your adult
  children. The goal of confrontation
  is a loving, healthy lifestyle and
  relationship.[24]

- Make sure your comments exhibit
  true wisdom.[25]

- Take time to consider the exact
  words (and tone of voice) you use
  when speaking to them.[26]

- Once you have made your position
  clear, don't keep bringing up the
  subject.

When we are disappointed in our children's behavior, we must live with the burden of incomplete relationships until they
are ready to repent of their failure. This
means not talking about your child's failures to others and not sitting around
allowing the situation to eat away at you.

No matter what, parents cannot do four things when deeply disappointed by adult children:

1. *Parents cannot give up.*
2. *Parents cannot cut off all contact.*
3. *Parents cannot negate the wrong choices.*
4. *Parents cannot reverse the damages.*

Forgiveness is not the end goal when adult children fail; it's the first step in reestablishing or maintaining a relationship.

When It's Time to Push Them Out of the Nest

You might be wondering, *Aren't there times to say* no *to my adult children? Aren't there times to boot them out?* In a word: yes. You might have to refuse to let your adult child move in or you may have to ask him to leave if he:

- refuses to recognize your authority over the home;
- is physically abusive;
- is verbally destructive;
- abuses or is addicted to drugs or alcohol and refuses treatment;

_____ තතත _____

"I have an adult son who has never moved from home. He will be 30 this month, and I've been a single mother since he was 5. He has had various jobs, but the longest one he kept was part time, 10 years ago. I keep waiting for him to grow up, but I don't think he wants to. I cannot see a time in the future where I can imagine him on his own. I feel resentful and guilty at the same time. He seems to live with a set of standards, or rather lack of standards, that are completely different from the way he was raised."

- is using your home merely to avoid facing an unresolved situation (such as marriage difficulties);
- repeatedly steals or destroys your belongings.

What if your child doesn't do any of those things, but she's not motivated to grow up and move out on her own? Should you let her live with you indefinitely? As the homeowner, you have every right to expect your grown child to contribute to the household expenses and follow the rules you set. But you also have the right to expect her to eventually move out and make a life of her own. Dr. James Dobson, psychologist and author, has some advice for parents whose kids are stuck in a holding pattern.

Question: Our 24-year-old daughter came home from college and moved back into

*her old bedroom. Now, three years later,
she's still there. She doesn't work, she has
no ambition or direction, and she seems
perfectly content to freeload on her dad
and me. I know she ought to get on with
her life, but what can I do? I can't just
force her out, can I?*

Answer: Your daughter is not alone. Millions of young adults are living at home and loving it. They have no intention of growing up—and why should they? The nest is just too comfortable there. Food is prepared. Clothes are laundered, and the bills are paid. There's no incentive to face the cold world of reality, and they are determined not to budge. Some, like your daughter, even refuse to work.

I know it's difficult to dislodge a homebound son or daughter. They're like furry little puppies who hang

around the back door waiting for a
saucer of warm milk. But to let them
stay year after year, especially if they're
not pursuing career goals, is to cultivate
irresponsibility and dependency. That's
not love, even though it may feel like it.
There comes the time when you must
gently but forthrightly hand the reins
over to your adult daughter and force
her to stand on her own. I think it's
time to help her pack.

Giving a shove to a 27-year-old
woman may seem cruel at the time,
but I encourage you to consider
emancipating her. The parental gravy
train probably should go around the
bend. If that never happens, lasting
characteristics of dependency and
immaturity may ensue.

I suggest you sit down and talk to
your daughter, explaining why the

time has come for her to make a life of her own. Set a deadline, perhaps two or three weeks ahead, and begin preparing for it. Then give her a big hug, a promise of prayers, and send her on her way.[27]

Conclusion

Many of us watched the men's 400-meter race in the 1992 Summer Olympic Games in Barcelona. For a few moments, we forgot who won, and all of us watched, instead, British runner Derek Redmond. He was the one who violently pulled a hamstring muscle and collapsed to the track midway through the race. With the crush of disappointment and the piercing agony of pain written on his face, he struggled to get to his feet. Olympic officials hurried to help him off the track. But with tears rolling down his face, he shoved them aside.

The pain was so great he stumbled, hopped, and hobbled. It looked as if there was no way he could go on. The race was long over when the crowd began to cheer for Derek. Even with their encouragement, it appeared he couldn't do it. Pain was overcoming the will to go on.

Then an older man illegally broke through the ranks of people around the track. He walked right up to Derek and grabbed him around the chest. Derek threw his arm over the man's shoulder.

That was not an official trying to get Derek off the track. That man was Derek Redmond's father. Still in anguish, Derek completed the race to a standing ovation.

Few of us will have sons or daughters who will compete in the Olympics. But it's almost assured that our children will face tough times. Then it will be our turn to fight our way through the crowd, lift them up, and help them cross their finish line.

That's what parenting is all about, no matter what the age of your child.

Notes

1. Frances K. and Calvin Goldscheider, "Family Structure and Conflict: Nest-Leaving Expectations of Young Adults and their Parents," *Journal of Marriage and the Family*, 51, February 1989, 87.
2. Allan Schnaiberg and Sheldon Goldenberg, "From Empty Nest to Crowded Nest: The Dynamics of Incompletely-Launched Young Adults," *Social Problems*, 36:3, June 1989, 231.
3. Ibid., 232.
4. Web site: www.seniorjournal.com/news/housing/4-06-29 survey.htm
5. Web site: Moneycentral.usa.com/content/collegeandFamily/raisekids/P98891.asp
6. Web site: Spiked-online.com/articles/00000006DE8D.htm
7. Ibid.
8. Ibid.
9. Ibid.
10. William S. Aquilino and Khalil R. Supple, "Parent-Child Relations and Parents' Satisfaction with Living Arrangements When Adult

Children Live at Home," *Journal of Marriage and the Family*, 53, February 1991, 24.

11. Ibid., 25.
12. Aquilino and Supple, "Parent-Child Relations," 25.
13. See James 3:17.
14. See Luke 15:11-32.
15. See Luke 15:12-13.
16. See Romans 3:23.
17. See Ezekiel 18:4.
18. See Jeremiah 17:9.
19. See Luke 15:13.
20. See Luke 15:17-18.
21. See Luke 15:20-24.
22. See 2 Timothy 4:2.
23. See Galatians 6:1-2.
24. See 2 Thessalonians 3:15.
25. See James 3:17.
26. See Ephesians 4:29, Colossians 4:6.
27. James Dobson, *Complete Marriage and Family Home Reference Guide* (Carol Stream, Ill.: Tyndale House, 2000), 255-56.

Resources

BOOKS

Cloud, Dr. Henry and Dr. John Townsend. *Boundaries: When to Say Yes, When to Say No to Take Control of Your Life*. Grand Rapids, Mich.: Zondervan, 2002.

Cloud, Dr. Henry and Dr. John Townsend. *Boundaries Workbook*. Grand Rapids, Mich.: Zondervan, 1995.

Peel, Kathy. *Family for Life: How to Have Happy, Healthy Relationships with Your Adult Children*. New York: McGraw Hill, 2003.

Sande, Ken with Tom Raabe. *Peacemaking for Families: A Biblical Guide to Managing Conflict in Your Home*. Carol Stream, Ill.: Tyndale House, 2002.

Smalley, Dr. Gary, Michael Smalley and Robert S. Paul. *The DNA of Relationships: Discover How You Are Designed for Satisfying Relationships*. Carol Stream, Ill.: Tyndale House, 2004.

ORGANIZATIONS

Crown Financial Ministries
P.O. Box 100
Gainesville, GA 30503-0100
(800) 722-1976; www.crown.org

Focus on the Family
8605 Explorer Dr.
Colorado Springs, CO 80920
(800) AFAMILY [(800) 232-6459]; www.family.org

Dr. Bill Maier is Focus on the Family's vice president and psychologist in residence. Dr. Maier received his master's and doctoral degrees from the Rosemead School of Psychology at Biola University in La Mirada, California. A child and family psychologist, Dr. Maier hosts the national "Weekend Magazine" radio program and the "Family Minute with Dr. Bill Maier." He also acts as a media spokesperson for Focus on the Family on a variety of family-related issues. He and his wife, Lisa, have been married for more than seven years and have two children.

Stephen Bly has authored 100 books, hundreds of articles, and has over one million books in print. He speaks at colleges, schools, churches, seminars, and conferences across the U.S. and Canada and has been a guest on numerous television and radio programs, including Dr. James Dobson's *Focus on the Family*. He is a pastor and mayor of a mountain town in Idaho where he and his wife, Janet, reside. The Blys have three grown sons—all of whom have married and left home.

FOCUS ^{ON}_{THE} FAMILY®

Welcome to the family!

Whether you purchased this book, borrowed it, or received it as a gift, we're glad you're reading it. It's just one of the many helpful, encouraging, and biblically based resources produced by Focus on the Family for people in all stages of life.

Focus began in 1977 with the vision of one man, Dr. James Dobson, a licensed psychologist and author of numerous best-selling books on marriage, parenting, and family. Alarmed by the societal, political, and economic pressures that were threatening the existence of the American family, Dr. Dobson founded Focus on the Family with one employee and a once-a-week radio broadcast aired on 36 stations.

Now an international organization reaching millions of people daily, Focus on the Family is dedicated to preserving values and strengthening and encouraging families through the life-changing message of Jesus Christ.

Focus on the Family Magazines

These faith-building, character-developing publications address the interests, issues, concerns, and challenges faced by every member of your family from preschool through the senior years.

| Focus on the Family Citizen™ U.S. news issues | Focus on the Family Clubhouse Jr.™ Ages 4 to 8 | Focus on the Family Clubhouse™ Ages 8 to 12 | Breakaway® Teen guys | brio® Teen girls 12 to 16 | Brio & Beyond® Teen girls 16 to 19 | Plugged In® Reviews movies, music, TV |

FOR MORE INFORMATION

 Online:
Log on to www.family.org
In Canada, log on to
www.focusonthefamily.ca

 Phone:
Call toll free: (800) A-FAMILY
In Canada, call toll free:
(800) 661-9800

More Great Resources
from Focus on the Family®

Wild Child, Waiting Mom
by Karilee Hayden and Wendi Hayden English

Wendi English and her mother Karilee Hayden chronicle their parallel stories of Wendi's pursuit of "freedom" at all costs. Wendi turned away from the values and love of her family. But in the midst of it all, God brought Karilee the gift of hope that enabled her to pray for and love her daughter.

Help! Someone I Love Is Depressed
by Archibald Hart, Ph.D.
Dr. Bill Maier, General Editor

Is someone you love depressed? You're not alone. Depression is so epidemic it's often called the "common cold" of the emotions. Understanding depression and how it affects people is the key to helping them. This book offers solid advice for helping someone who's depressed.

Help! Someone I Know Has a Problem with Porn
by Jim Vigorito, Ph.D.
Dr. Bill Maier, General Editor

Does someone you know have a problem with Porn? Today's technologies have opened even more venues for pornography access. You may know someone who is caught in the porn trap. This book offers practical advice on several key topics.

FOR MORE INFORMATION

 Online:
Log on to www.family.org
In Canada, log on to www.focusonthefamily.ca.

FOCUS
on the Family®

 Phone:
Call toll free: (800) A-FAMILY
In Canada, call toll free: (800) 661-9800.

BP06XP1